BORTHWICK INSTITUTE FOR ARCH
UNIVERSITY OF YORK

Verses and Fragments: Poems of the Great War

by
John Stanley Purvis

Edited by
Professor Sue Mendus

BORTHWICK TEXTS AND STUDIES 46

Acknowledgements

The poems published here are taken from a notebook belonging to John Stanley Purvis, lodged at the Borthwick Institute for Archives at the University of York. I am deeply indebted to the staff at the Borthwick, all of whom have been knowledgeable, helpful, and friendly in equal measure. It is always a pleasure to work with them, and I have been privileged to have the benefit of their expertise. I extend my warmest thanks, and my sincerest admiration, to them all.

Special thanks are owed to two members of staff at the Borthwick: Lydia Dean and Gary Brannan. Lydia has been tireless in her support of this project. She has responded swiftly and efficiently to my many requests for help and has remained cheerful in the face of my most incoherent requests. I genuinely could not have managed without her. Gary, as Keeper of Archives and Research Collections, has also been unfailingly supportive of the project, and has offered invaluable advice on permissions, publication, publicity, and much else. It has been a real, and rare, privilege to work with them.

My work on Purvis's poems was first presented as the Sheldon Memorial Lecture at the University of York in 2021. I am grateful to the Sheldon Memorial Trust for inviting me to give the talk in the first instance, and to David Foster and Sarah Sheils for their continuing interest and encouragement.

Finally, the path to this publication has been made much smoother thanks to Rev. Elizabeth Jackson. When I first considered publishing the poems, it was not known who was able to give permission for their publication. Through pure chance (and through Gary Brannan!) I discovered that the right person was Rev Elizabeth Jackson. Liz, as I now know her, has been immensely generous with her time, with her knowledge of the Purvis family, and with the family documents she has inherited. Through her generosity, the Borthwick now has yet more material in the Purvis collection, and I am confident that this material will prove to be fertile ground for researchers in the future. I thank her most warmly for her help and for her friendship.

Sue Mendus
University of York
January 2023.

Contents

Introduction

The poems published here have been transcribed from a handwritten notebook which is lodged in the Borthwick Institute for Archives at the University of York. The notebook belonged to John Stanley Purvis (Canon Purvis of York Minster ref PURVIS/7/3/4/1), and its frontispiece bears the title: *Verses and Fragments: Written at Cambridge, Cranleigh and in France*. Each poem in the notebook is dated: the first, entitled 'On the Cheviots: August', was written in September 1912, and the last, entitled 'In Memoriam: Fragments', was written in July 1917. These, then, are poems of the Great War. They were written at Cambridge, where Purvis took a degree in History, at Cranleigh, where he was a school teacher, and in France, where he served on the Western Front.

All but two of the poems in Purvis's notebook are published here for the first time. The exceptions are 'Chance Memory' and 'The Tourists' Complete Guide to the Battlefields: High Wood'. 'Chance Memory' was published in *The Daily News* on 23 June 1916, under the name 'Philip Johnson', and 'High Wood' was published in *The Nation* on 16 February 1918 under the name 'Philip Johnston'. However, both are the work of John Stanley Purvis. They are in the *Verses and Fragments* notebook, and they are written in Purvis's hand.

These few, bare facts about the notebook and the poems give rise to many questions: why did Purvis publish only two of the very large number of poems he wrote, and why did he not publish them under his own name? Why was he so secretive about his identity as the author of 'Chance Memory' and 'High Wood'? And why did his sister, Hilda Purvis, feel free to disclose the fact that he was their author only after his death in 1968? The questions would, perhaps, be less puzzling had Purvis been, in general, a private or retiring person. But he was not. On the contrary, he was a very prominent figure in the city of York, and a distinguished canon and prebendary at York Minster. He had a significant career in public life and was a very well-known and highly regarded citizen of York. The short summary of his career given in the next section cannot do justice to the full range of Purvis's public and professional activities, but I hope it will serve to give a flavour of his life and work, and to emphasise how puzzling it is that this very public man was also a very private, indeed a very secretive, poet.[1]

---

1   Much more information about Purvis, and especially about his scholarly and ecclesiastical work, can be found in the Borthwick Institute for Archives at the University of York. Information about his army career, and especially about his service in the Great War, is held at the Green Howards Museum, Richmond, North Yorkshire.

John Stanley Purvis: The Public Life[2]

John Stanley Purvis, the first child of Major John Bowlt Purvis and Charlotte Annie Purvis, was born in Bridlington on 9 May 1890. He attended Bridlington Grammar School and went from there as an Exhibitioner to St Catharine's College, Cambridge, where he studied History. On graduating from Cambridge in 1912, Purvis took up a post as teacher, and subsequently Housemaster, at Cranleigh School, where he remained until 1938. His time at Cranleigh was interrupted only by his service in the First World War, of which more will be said later.

In 1933 Purvis was ordained as deacon and subsequently as priest. In 1938 he resigned from his post at Cranleigh and returned to his native Yorkshire to pursue what was to be a long and distinguished ecclesiastical career. His first position was as rector of Goodmanham, in what is now the East Riding of Yorkshire. In 1941, he moved on to become vicar of Old Malton, and then, in 1954, he became Canon of Strensall. In addition to these ecclesiastical roles, Purvis also did a huge amount of historical work: he wrote extensively about religious matters and had a deep interest in church history and in church archives[3]. In 1939 he was appointed the first archivist to the Archbishop of York, and throughout the 1940s he was a staunch supporter of the campaign to establish a university in the city – believing, along with a number of other distinguished citizens, that York remained incomplete while it lacked a university[4].

In May 1953 the Borthwick Institute of Historical Research (now the Borthwick Institute for Archives) was opened with much publicity and to great fanfare. At the opening, the banners proclaimed, 'Making York a World Centre of History'. John Stanley Purvis was appointed the first Director of the Borthwick, and it was not long before he was travelling to the United States, giving lectures and publicising the important historical and archival work that was being done at York[5]. All this was part

---

2   Material for this section is taken from the York Civic Trust website, and from the obituary of Purvis published in the *Yorkshire Archaeological Journal*, xlii (1971), pp.520-522.

3   See, for instance, his book *The Dissolution of Bridlington Priory*, 1923.

4   See Katherine Webb, *City of Our Dreams: J B Morrell and the Shaping of Modern York*, Borthwick Texts and Studies, 2019, pp. 128-142. See, too, J S Purvis *Towards a University*, Borthwick Institute for Archives.

5   *City of Our Dreams*, op. cit. p.137.

of a sustained, and lengthy, campaign to ensure that York was given the university which its citizens felt it deserved[6].

In short, then, Purvis was a very distinguished scholar, writer, and historian: he worked extensively on ecclesiastical subjects, and published a number of scholarly historical works, including a history of St Anthony's Hall, which was the first home of the Borthwick Institute. In 1951, he wrote the first modern script for the revival of the York Mystery Plays, and he expanded the text of the Mystery Plays for their 1957 production. In addition, and to mention just a few distinctions, he was: Fellow of the Royal Society of Antiquaries, Fellow of the Royal Historical Society, and President of the Yorkshire Archaeological Society. In 1958, his work received due acknowledgement in the Queen's Birthday Honours, when he was made an OBE for services to historical scholarship.

John Stanley Purvis: The Private Poet

However, this very public story was not all for, as has been noted, Purvis was also a very private poet. Here, too, he wrote extensively, but published only two of his poems, and those two were published pseudonymously. Moreover, there is reason to believe that his silence about the poems was deliberate – that it was, in fact, not mere silence, but secrecy. The evidence for this is provided by Purvis's sister, Hilda Purvis, and the story is this[7]:

In his 1970 autobiography, *Good Morning, Good People*, the author Ernest Raymond wrote:

> In 1916, having recently escaped from the mud and filth of Gallipoli, I was with my brigade in the Sinai Desert, where we were slowly laying a railway through the sands towards Gaza, making straight in the desert a highway to Jerusalem. And one day, I chanced upon an old, tattered copy of the *Daily News* and read in it a brief poem whose final couplet seemed to me – I have said this in articles and on platforms and in private talks for over half a century – to capture an English soldier's native patriotism with simpler or more perfect words than any other lines in that luxuriant yield

---

6   In this context, it is worth noting that the University of York, unlike the other 'new' universities established in the 1960s, came about through the efforts of private citizens, not (or not primarily) as a result of council action. See Katherine Webb *City of Our Dreams,* op. cit. p.140.

7   Much of the information here has been taken from the Steyning Museum website: http:// steyningmuseum.org.uk/purvis.htm.

of poetry which sprang from the First World War. Ever a lover of the bare, sweeping downs of Sussex which find their crown in the ring of noble trees on Chanctonbury, I was caught, I suppose, by the title *From Steyning to the Ring*. I read the poem once – twice or thrice maybe – and have been word perfect in it ever since. It was printed over the name 'Philip Johnson', and never from that day in 1916 until two mornings ago, in 1969, fifty-three years later, have I known who Philip Johnson was, or heard of him[8].

In fact, Raymond's memory deceives him, for the poem is called 'Chance Memory'. It was published in the *Daily News* on 23 June 1916, and it appears in the *Verses and Fragments* notebook. It runs:

> I can't forget the lane that goes from Steyning to the Ring
> In summer time, and on the Downs how larks and linnets sing
> High in the sun. The wind comes off the sea, and Oh the air! —
> I never knew till now that life in old days was so fair.
> But now I know it in this filthy rat-infested ditch,
> When every shell must kill or spare, and God alone knows which.
> And I am made a beast of prey and this trench is my lair: -
> My God! I never knew till now that those days were so fair.
> And we assault in half an hour, and ... it's a silly thing,
> I can't forget the lane that goes from Steyning to the Ring.

For more than half a century Ernest Raymond had publicly declared his admiration for this poem, but he could find no record of, or information about, its author, Philip Johnson, until one day in 1969 when he received a letter from Miss Hilda Purvis of Bridlington. She wrote:

> Since the death of my brother, Canon J S Purvis, in December I have been searching the family news cuttings albums to find an article which you wrote in the Sunday Times of 22 May 1927. My mother preserved our copy at the time for she knew the pen name Philip Johnson was that of her elder son John Stanley. Through the years I have often thought that I should like to reveal to you the real name of the author who wrote this poem.

---

8   Ernest Raymond *Good Morning, Good People: An Autobiography Past and Present*, London, Cassell, 1970, *p.45*.

Drawing of Steyning by JS Purvis.

The words were sent without my brother's knowledge to the Press by his friend, a Quaker doctor, serving with the Red Cross.... Please forgive me if I have bored you with these reminiscences but I have always wanted to uncover the anonymity of my noble brother 'Philip Johnson' and to thank you for the words in your article which gave so much pleasure to my mother and to me[9].

So, the mysterious poet, Philip Johnson, was in fact John Stanley Purvis, and it is clear from his sister's letter that the poem was initially published without his knowledge or approval, and that once it had been published, he did not wish to be identified publicly as its author. Hence Hilda Purvis's decision to wait until after his death, at the end of 1968, before writing to Ernest Raymond and revealing her brother's identity.

Why Purvis did not wish his identity to be revealed is a matter for speculation, and it is possible that the answer will never be known. What we can do, however, is to examine the ways in which the poems, taken as a whole, track his life and experiences during the years of the Great War. We can see how the tone and temper of the poems changed as the war unfolded, and we can, perhaps, discern something of the changing mood of the poet himself.

In the next section, I will say something about John Stanley Purvis's career as a soldier of the Great War, and I will identify some crucial junctures at which his life seems, at least, to illuminate his poetry. Obviously, after so many years have passed, much of this must be speculative. Nonetheless, I hope that, by identifying some seminal moments in his life, and by examining the poetry he composed at those moments, we will be able to gain a better understanding of the reasons he had for composing the poems, and also of the reasons he may have had for keeping the fact of his authorship a closely guarded secret.

John Stanley Purvis: Soldier of the Great War

Born in May 1890, John Stanley Purvis was the first child of John Bowlt Purvis and Charlotte Annie Purvis. Their second child, George Bell Purvis, was born on 1 September 1892, and their third child, and only daughter, Hilda Mary Purvis – the author of the letter to Ernest Raymond – was born five years later, on 17 December 1897.

In 1913 John Stanley, who was teaching at Cranleigh School on the South Downs, received a commission in the Royal West Surrey Regiment. Two years later,

---

9   Op.cit. p.46.

in 1915, he transferred to the 5th Battalion, Alexandra Princess of Wales's Own Yorkshire Regiment (commonly known as the Green Howards), where he served with his father, John Bowlt Purvis, and brother, George Bell Purvis, in France and in Flanders[10]. John Stanley's brother, George Bell Purvis, was commissioned to the 5th Battalion of the Green Howards in June 1914, and when the battle of the Somme began in July 1916, both brothers saw action on the Western Front. Crucially, both were in the front line at the notorious attack on High Wood in September 1916. High Wood was, in fact, John Stanley's first experience of close combat, and it proved to be hugely traumatic for him, both physically and emotionally. The first time he went 'over the top', on 15 September 1916, he was badly injured and sent back to Britain, suffering from what was then known as 'shell shock'[11]. It seems likely that he never fully recovered from the experience and although he returned to the Western Front, it was not to engage in further front-line battle. His experience and his trauma were, of course, far from unique: the First World War was, and remains, notorious for its brutality, its industrial death toll, and its almost casual disregard for human life. But even in that exceptionally bloody and brutal war ('the war to end war'), High Wood had the distinction of being a very special 'Hell'.

Briefly put, the circumstances surrounding and leading up to the battle for High Wood are as follows[12]: what is usually referred to as 'the battle of the Somme' was in fact a series of distinct battles waged in northern France over a four-and-a-half-month period from 1 July to 18 November 1916. The battle for High Wood's 75 acres began on July 14, 1916 and raged nearly continuously for 64 days. It opened with a disastrous British cavalry charge and ended after the abortive first use of tanks on 15 September.

Over and over again, accounts of the battle for High Wood emphasise the truly appalling conditions that prevailed, the catastrophic decisions that were taken, and the huge loss of life that was sustained, but what was distinctive of, and ultimately disastrous about, the battle for High Wood was the British decision to use tanks for

---

10   Obituary *Yorkshire Archaeological Journal,* 1971, pp.520.

11   The Borthwick collection contains a small notebook belonging to Charlotte Purvis, in which she records her son's return from the Front 'with shell shock'.

12   There are, of course, many accounts of the war on the Somme. This account draws on Lyn Macdonald's excellent book, *Somme,* Penguin, Harmondsworth, 1983, and on the *Owlcation* website: https://owlcation.com/humanities/World-War-1-History-High-Wood-The-Sommes-75-Acres-of-Hell

George and John Stanley Purvis in uniform

the first time. Initially, this decision seemed vindicated, as the movement of tanks across the battlefield terrified the German soldiers and seemed to signal the dawn of a swift and convincing victory for the British. Lance-Corporal Len Lovell of the 6th Battalion, King's Own Yorkshire Light Infantry wrote:

> It was marvellous. The tanks went on, rolling and bobbing and swaying in and out of shell holes, climbing over trees as easy as kiss your hand! We were awed! ...The Jerries waited until our tank was only a few yards away and then fled – or hoped to! The tank just shot them down and the machine-gun post, the gun itself, the dead and wounded who hadn't been able to run, just disappeared. The tank went right over them. We would have danced for joy if it had been possible out there. It seemed so easy! ... We were elated[13].

Soon, however, elation turned to terror, as it became clear that the terrain was wholly unsuited to tanks, and that the decision to deploy them had been, in effect, a decision to offer up thousands of young men as sacrificial lambs on the altar of the British war effort. In her detailed and deeply unsettling book, *Somme*, Lyn Macdonald writes:

> Of course, the tanks should never have been ordered into High Wood at all and so the Commander of the 47th Division had told GHQ in the frankest of terms. In the opinion of General Sir Charles Barter, even a child could have seen that the pitted, fought-over ground, the upturned trees, the stockade of jagged stumps, the morass of craters and shell-holes lying lip to lip, were insurmountable obstacles to any vehicle, regardless of its might, regardless of the brilliance of its trials over open country. He had not succeeded in convincing the powers that be. They patiently pointed out that the British and German lines lay too close to each other in High Wood for the artillery to bombard and crush the enemy defences. The tanks must do the job. The powers-that-be had not seen for themselves the conditions in High Wood. The General had. Let the tanks go round the perimeter of the wood, he suggested, and the wood itself could then be crushed as easily as a walnut in the jaws of a nutcracker. The General had been over-ruled, but he had been right. Only one of the tanks had been

---

13   As reported in Lyn Macdonald *Somme*, Penguin, Harmondsworth, 1993, pp.286-7. John Stanley Purvis's sketches and photographs of High Wood, including photographs of the tanks, are to be found in the Green Howards Museum, Richmond, North Yorkshire.

able to move forward through the wood and, before long, it had stuck. .....
In two months, High Wood had cost the lives of several thousand men.
Most battalions were reduced to half their strength long before the day (15
September) ended. Most battalions had lost their colonels. Some had lost
every single officer[14].

This – the Hell of High Wood – was John Stanley Purvis's introduction to war.
Both he and his brother, George, were in the front line and both went 'over the
top' on that dreadful day, 15th September 1916. As was noted earlier, John Stanley
was injured and returned to England, and to Cranleigh, where he spoke to the boys
about his experiences in battle, and where he wrote some of the poems published
in this volume. One such poem is *Schoolboys, 1916*, which was written at Cranleigh
in September of 1916 and which opens with the lines:

> You question eagerly to learn of us,
> Who come and go
> From war to you and back to war again,
> And feeling there is much we will not tell,
> You seek to know the worst things of that hell.
> O be content to leave the matter so;
> Thank God you do not know.

These lines, written shortly after Purvis's return from High Wood, stand in stark
contrast to some of his earlier poems which, if not quite jingoistic, are certainly full
of optimism, and of patriotism. Contrast the opening lines of *Schoolboys* with the
opening lines of the earlier poem, *Valedictory*, also written at Cranleigh, but before
High Wood – in December 1915:

> Now by the land which our forefathers won,
> Now by the work which in this land they wrought,
> Let us continue what they have begun,
> Let us so fight for England as they fought.

That said, it must also be conceded that the evidence is not all one-way, for there
are also early poems which emphasise the waste of life – and especially of young
life – that is characteristic of war. Nonetheless, when war became a lived reality
for Purvis, his attitude seems, understandably, to have hardened, and his initial
optimism to have turned to pessimism, even to cynicism.

---

14   Lyn MacDonald *Somme*, op.cit., pp. 296-7.

Having survived the Hell that was High Wood, and having spent time recuperating at Cranleigh, Purvis returned to France and to the war, in March 1917. However, it was only a short time after that, in June 1917, that news was brought of his brother's death in action. The Yorkshire Regiment *Remembrance* website records that: 'In the summer of 1917 [George Bell Purvis] was due to return to England as an instructor at a machine gun school, but during the Battle of Messines he was killed in action on June 8th, 1917, aged 24, as he was reconnoitring for new gun positions'[15].

For John Stanley, already deeply damaged by his own war experiences, George's death must have been a massive blow. The *Verses and Fragments* notebook contains a loose-leaf manuscript of 'High Wood' on the back of which is the bare inscription, in Purvis's hand, 'G B P killed June 8, 1917. News brought June 16'.

'High Wood', whose full title is 'The Tourists' Complete Guide to the Battlefields: High Wood', anticipates the day when the Western Front will be a mere holiday destination – a stopping off point for inquisitive and voyeuristic tourists, wishing to see the 'killing fields' of the Somme. It is written as if spoken by a tour guide, and contains the lines:

You are requested kindly not to touch
Or take away the Company's property
As souvenirs, you will find we have on sale
A large variety, all guaranteed.
As I was saying, all is as it was,
This is an unknown British officer,
The tunic having lately rotted off.
Please follow me – this way...
        the path sir, please.

The poem is dated 'Humbercamps 2.6.17', suggesting that it was written just days before George's death at Messines.

These, then, are the circumstances surrounding the composition of *Verses and Fragments*. They are the poems of a young schoolteacher, destined to see his brother, his pupils, and many of his friends, die on the Western Front. They are also the poems of a young man destined to become a canon at York Minster, the archivist to the Archbishop of York, the translator of the York Mystery Plays and, as we have seen, much else besides. But underlying, and pre-dating, all his many public, academic, and ecclesiastical achievements was John Stanley Purvis's

---

15 https://www.ww1-yorkshires.org.uk.

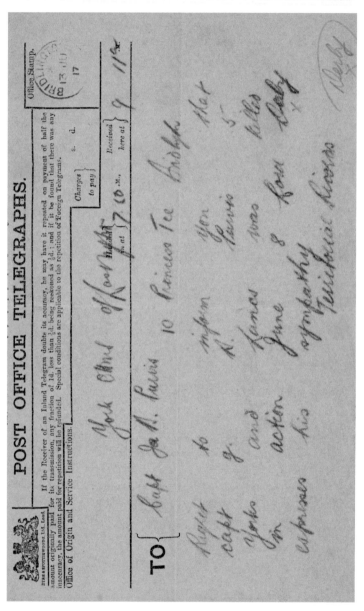

Telegram, giving news of the death of George Purvis, 1917

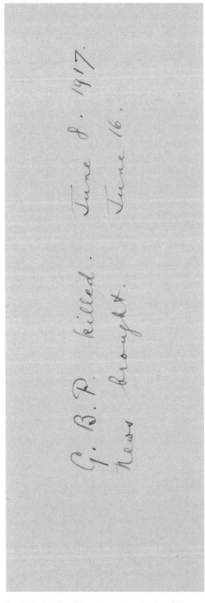

Notes after 'High Wood' marking the death of George Purvis

experience as a soldier of the Great War, and there is reason to think that, for him, as for so many other young men, the Great War was a supreme test of faith[16].

The final poem in *Verses and Fragments* is entitled *In Memoriam*. It is dated 'July 1917' and it reads:

> I will not grieve him as untimely dead,
> Nor yet upbraid
> The Hand that took him; I can yet believe
> That unafraid
> He faced the instant peril that his head
> Bowed not, nor did the level of his eyes
> Tremble or fall
> Before the menace of Death's fronting gaze
> And best of all,
> That as a fighter to the last he lies.
>
> He might have lived, but that he did not choose
> For that great day
> To leave the men whose friend and leader he;
> The better way
> So gain is most when most he seems to lose.

It is hard to resist the thought that the subject of this final poem is John Stanley's brother, George Bell Purvis, who had been killed so very recently at Messines. By July of 1917, news of George's death had been brought to the Purvis family and, in a letter to the Purvis family, the Brigadier General wrote: 'I personally would have followed him anywhere and I know this was the feeling of the other officers and the men of the company'.

Years later, long after the end of the Great War, John Stanley Purvis visited his brother's grave at Kleine Vierstaat. He photographed and sketched the war cemetery and his brother's grave and headstone many times. Unsurprisingly, the tragedy of his brother's death, at the age of just 24, seems to have haunted him down the years and, for myself, I do not think it fanciful to suppose that the poems in *Verses and Fragments* were simply too personal and too painful to be offered up for publication. Or, even, to be publicly acknowledged.

---

16   Given that Purvis went on to take holy orders, we must conclude that his faith survived the test.

Grave and headstone of George Purvis at Kleine Vierstaat

Crucifix at Courcelles

The final poem in this volume is not to be found in the *Verses and Fragments* notebook. It is a separate poem, written on a single piece of paper, and it was very kindly given to me by Revd. Elizabeth Jackson, whose parents were cousins of John Stanley Purvis, and who inherited many of the papers, documents, and drawings left by him. These papers have been generously lodged at the Borthwick Institute for Archives at the University of York and are therefore available for reference and research. The poem is called 'Crucifix at Courcelles'. It is dated '6.5.17'and it compares the death of soldiers in the Great War with the death of Christ on the Cross. The final stanza reads:

> On either side, no thief, but slaughtered friends,
> Which his hands find,
> And rats. But more. Not helpless only; blind,
> — O Christ! — blind, blind.
> An agony which no ninth hour death ends.

The horror of war and the agony of death are graphically described here as they are in so many of the poems in the *Verses and Fragments* notebook. Perhaps the horror and the agony help to explain Purvis's need for privacy in the matter of his verse, and perhaps they also illuminate the test of faith which, for so many, was the Great War.

Whatever the truth about that, the poems can now speak for themselves.

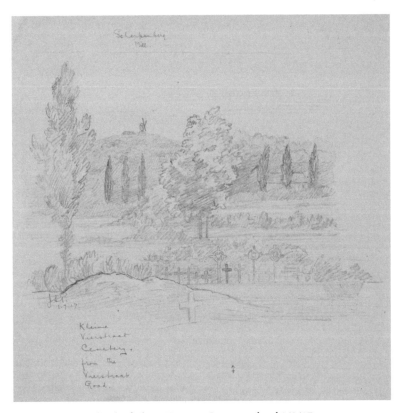

Sketch of Kleine Vierstaat Cemetery, dated 1/9/17

Verses and Fragments;
Poems of the Great War
John Stanley Purvis

Written at Cambridge, Cranleigh, and in France

On the Cheviots
August

Oh good! To walk upon the crests of hills,
Look down into those blue steep valleys there
So narrow, raise the eyes and see the heave
Of these bare sunny slopes[1]; the wide expanse
That cheers the eye and raises up the heart.
Hills to be climbed; such hills to look upon
With blue & purple slopes[2], & far below
The little stream half-buried in the depth:
And then again look up and see the stretch
Of endless slopes, and rising over all
Crest upon crest of wild untrodden hills
Ever & ever higher, and the sun
That gives its strength to theirs and makes them glad;
Until the joy that fills their utmost limb
Mounts into mine, and their strength makes me strong.

There is a noble big simplicity
About these hills. See now yon fellow there
Who heaves his smooth round solitary side
So high, and smiles i'the sun: is he not like
Some big broad minded man who stands and smiles
On all men, whom no little things annoy.
Of large slow temper, strong and unafraid?
A man might sit him down alone & think —
Perhaps his only friend for company,
If he be silent, just they two alone –
And let the hills talk to him; first, of earth,
Mere happiness of living: all the good
That is on earth, and how much better here
Is life than in the noisy filthy towns
Where hurry and clang – in such calm solitude
The very thought's a blot. No: rather look

---

1   'hills' deleted in manuscript.
2   'depths' deleted in manuscript.

Upon the hills & let them soothe the mind
And cleanse it. Their rest sinks in to the heart.
Their calm, their endless strength.
            The breath comes deep:
The comfort of the limbs sets free the mind
To wander in those purple distances –
The mountains lead it upwards, as they rise
Into the pure thin lofty fields of air,
And ever on, from height to loftier height,
Till things are reached which are too great for thought,
Which no man ever has expressed in words
But gasps and stumbles, even as the mind
Stands all aghast because they are so great,
So wide and overpow'ring: then the soul
Seems loosened from the body, stands above
The man, as he were dead, and is at one
With all infinity.
            The silent hills,
A winter sunset on the lonely wolds,
Deep silent starlight nights, the evening sea,
Some memory of School or friends, a song,
Some dear thing lost so long ago – all these
Can so set free the soul.
            Yet he revives,
Comes back to earth, and grasps and struggles hard
To tell what awful raptures, holy things
The soul has half-seen in its ecstasy
And feels that life is changed for him henceforth.

And that hill there has stood so many years
When I was still unborn, and yet shall stand
So many years when I have left the earth,
To find the truth of all this half-concealed,
Half-realised awfulness.
            So many years:
Far down the past, the wide dim mournful past;
So many men came down this very road
And looked upon this hill before me now,

And they are gone for ever from the earth,
And who can say what trace of them remains?
So many, all forgotten. Oh what use
Pride and ambition? They had these as I.
What use to struggle when a little while
Will lay me even with them, forgotten too?

And all around me rises from the hills
The mighty symphony: for every hill—
Aye, every part of earth in every land,
But mostly here for me – has one great note,
One deep & awful organ-note, unvoiced,
Which no hand ever struck in Earthly key,
Which towers through the sky & swells its chords
In that eternal symphony which rings
Through all the earth, which I can almost hear,
Yet more has clearly heard. No man may tell
Or write it down – for that full sound would tear
The soul from out the body – while he lives.
It is the anthem of eternity.
The everlasting song of all the earth;
And I hear dimly echoes from the hills
And bow in worship, for they find in me
Some part that sounds in answer, height for height
So soon to be forgotten? I must live
To the full the life I have. And then perhaps
I yet shall leave some trace that I have lived
In some man better for my having lived.

O glorious Life! O loveliness of man!
O joy of earth, where is so much to love
O friendship, which gives men a sight of God!
"And from the mountain He came down".
          I heard,
"And went into the city". So must I.

09/12

A Song of Degrees

Brethren, with understanding eyes
We come within familiar walls,
We hear the Voice that ever calls
And see the ghostly past arise.

We value now what then was ours
Unvalued, friendship, love & life
Of fair acquaintance, glorious strife
On field & common, idle hours –

There was our nurture; yet unwise
To know our treasures: – power to live
And love a friend, the power to give
Our best in fullest sacrifice.

For here we cannot only take
Nor only act as laws decide;
Of all the school the highest pride
Is his who gave most for her sake.

In that same place which made us, where
Each one must mould the vase to be,
We leave, for every eye to see,
Our trace in changeless figure there;

The selfish aim is deepest guilt;
Love's work will last for good or ill
The School that builded us is still
For aye the School that we have built.

Cranleigh
Cranleighan
07/14

Memory

Here is no place for spending such a night,
A night of June so still & rare:
I cannot bear this sunset's calm delight
In city streets, with din and glare.
When I can hear so well the voices call,
See the white posts fade as the shadows fall,
And hear the whisper of the trees as tall,
By the North Field in sunset's dying light:
   And I not there.

O for the old Field once again tonight,
This precious hour of rose and gold;
To see the hills fade in the fading light
From Hascombe round to Winterfold.
High over Gatley's trees the evening star
Burns white. Yet still the clanging bell will jar
Too soon upon this peace. Youth's hour grows late:
Their joy than mine can have no longer date.
O for the North Field and a friend tonight –
   And I not there. And I not there!

Cranleighan
07/14

On facing page:
'The very whisper of the grass
Grass that ... [unreadable]

Autumn 1914

You who this autumn in the year of War
Go by the fields, hedges[3], look up & see
The lesson Autumn marks on hedge and tree.

The trees with leaves of flame are living fires
That burn the Heaven, as the houses burn
And churches fall in France with blazing spires.

Admire no more the red tints Autumn throws
In every hedge. Those drops are drops of blood,
Wrung from the martyrdom of Belgian woes.

Cranleighan
11/14

---

3   In MS 'woods' is deleted and replaced by 'hedges'.

Spring 1915

Spring is returning to the earth; this morn,
Even in these fields that war has rent & torn,
Fields ploughed by shells,
Even in that earth the green blade springs again,
And the bud swells.
The harvest of last Autumn trampled low
Gave all the sowing that these fields shall know.

The winter here has sowed a ghastlier grain,
A thousand thousand dead, thousands again,
Fall to the ground,
Lie stretched beneath these acres dumb and cold,
Heaped on each other, young men with the old,
Making no sound.
There in their ranks they lie, & no word said
Can bring the Spring to one of all these dead.

07/03/15

In Memoriam

PAGE BLANK IN NOTEBOOK

Cranleighan
03/15

Nought will it serve

Nought will it serve to think that o'er yon ground
Before your reeking trench, so deadly near,
In reeking trench your enemies are found,
Hot with your lust to kill, [4]chilled with your fear.
For it is hard to know, it was not hate,
But love of liberty that brought you here.

Nought will it serve to think when he is dead,
Thou mourning mother, when thy[5] son is slain,
That thou no more for aye shalt hear his tread:
No more: nought serve to wish him life again.
Think mother of the cause in which he died;
Think of the future's mothers saved from pain.

Thou in the trench, will it not serve to think
Upon the Man who died that we might live?
Thou mourning mother, nothing serve to think
That thou, like Mary, hadst a son to give.

14/08/15
10.30pm

---

4   'whipped' (in margin).
5   'your' (in margin).

Two Laws?

Bring not into this rabid world of war
The Crucified, to justify your cause.
Take to you, for His sweet and peaceful laws
The ancient Lord of Hosts, the ancient law.

Since thou hast taken up the sword, the life
Shall for its guidance have the sword's own law.
Live by the stern high chivalry of war,
Purged by the age-old fellowship of strife.

Worthy the company and life they spent
Who in all ages felt that strong constraint,
Cleansed of all weakness, faithful, continent,
Asked for no pity, died with no complaint.

15/08/15

The Awakening

The trumpets of the past ring clear and shrill
Out of the high grey dawn, on every hill.
Down in deep immemorial glades, the call
Sounds faint in distance. Where the blue shade lies
Beneath the ancient trees, the echoes fall,
A movement stirs, as misty forms arise.

The trumpets of the past sound on the hill;
Out on the Down the high grey dawn is chill.
Upon each barrow stands its inmate ghost,
The long dead chieftain resting from his strife:
On every hill ranks thick th'invisible host,
Roman & Dane & Norman, England's life
In ages past, the clarion calls from sleep.

Deep in the mystic gloom of ancient trees,
Waiting his time, the fabled king has lain:
Arthur, roused now from waiting, lives again;
Wondrous Excalibur is in his hand,
The hour is come to his beloved land,
And all the land's great dead are in his train.

To every quarter of Old England's bounds,
To all the shores of all the English seas,
The land is shaking with the tramp of men,
The air is shrill with trumpets; on the deep
Once more in pride & power warships sweep.
The dead have heard it & arise from sleep.

They see the England which they won and wrought,
They see the strength of England seek the fray.
Their blood still lives by which this land was bought,
This race is formed by their immortal clay.
Forth with our armies march the noble shades,
Eager to meet the call, to help, to inspire,
Stern to condemn if England's glory fades,
Glad to receive those who hand on the fire.

16/08/15

Valedictory
Departure for the Front

Now by the land which our forefathers won,
Now by the work which in this land they wrought,
Let us continue what they have begun,
Let us so fight for England as they fought.

They did not count the cost if England gained,
But reckoned all well spent for England's fame,
They did not grudge to die, if still unstained
Before the world was her beloved name.

Help us, ye noble dead, to think as high
Of England's ancient honour as you thought.
Live once again in us, that though we die,
Yet shall we fall no whit from what you wrought.

Ours is a hope as high, a joy as strong,
A field as spacious and a cause as rare;
England our theme in all the world; our song
The glory of England and our only care.

Cranleighan
12/15

O Envious Time

O Envious Time, whose over hasty gripe
Trembles to seize the richness of my prime,
For envy of my rare pleasure, waxing ripe
As life I me grows full with passing time.

Jealous that holding that which thou hast not,
Who dost surpass Aurora's spouse in years,
I, in whose veins the tide of youth is not,
Can face what is or shall be, without fears;

For triumph in the fullness & the pride
Of this fair world & all the life of men; –
I scorn the fated scythe. Though death betide,
Although tomorrow's dawn should end my span,
I could not tell, in years that equalled thine,
One half the joy in life that once was mine.

Cranleigh
13/11/15

Trench Warfare

Man cowers beneath the creatures of man's mind
In silly ditches he has dug for life,
Waiting his time to slaughter man. O blind
And bitter folly of such ridiculous strife!

13/11/15

Waste

The War lords lead their train of countless dead,
On whom the unending widow hosts attend;
Yet to the least of these, the life now shed
Was wonderful and precious to the end.

13/11/15

A Mood's Wish

O ten times worth ignoble life
Chain-galled by dull monotony,
To leave this base soul-penury
To seek a better end in strife: -

To seek such strife as courage won,
Where high endurance, owning not
Defeat's last hour, all self forgot,
Held on till the last sands were run: -

The strife where in the hostile scare
All wished for chances fortune flung,
But left to us a breathless tale
Of conflict such as Homer sung: -

To know that others yet unborn
Shall warm at my undying fray,
As still from Roncesvalles' day
I hear knight Roland's deathless horn

To end like Grenvile, or the Dane
Who held the bridge at Stamford fight,
To die, transfigured in the light
Of action, be a man again,

Where only manly actions live,
Where uninspired and base things fall;
To go, exulting, at the call,
Since life had nought so high to give.

Cranleigh
18/11/15

Dedication

I have fought for my soul, and have won it;
Eternally now
Is my fortune the fortune of England,
Which offers the vow
That we fight for her name and her freedom,
Though death be our gain,
To defend an ideal, a vision
Of peace and no pain,
Which shall flourish for ever and ever.
So death is not vain.

Cranleigh
18/11/15

[Untitled fragment]

The air is still & with the sun
All life is done
The trees no longer speak

But silent wait
What doom the evening brings.

To J.R.E.
Friendship

Old friend, not little does it count to me
That we, though oft apart,
Have still preserved our love, & still preserve
An understanding heart.
Each loving what is in the other, strange
Or common new or old,
Able to understand the motive, hear
The word that is not told: -

Still not afraid, if variation come
With our still ripening years,
That there shall come misunderstanding too,
Estrangement, doubts or fears.
Since it is in the spirit that we own
Our friendship's unity,
And in an equal love of noble things,
Of faith & charity.

We read together in the splendid lore
Of fellowship and love,
Together found the loveliness of life,
Man linked to God above.
Laughter and sorrow both alike we share,
Each to each strength shall lend;
So in the same communion let us still
Continue to the end.

Cranleigh
18/11/15

A Thought
Winter, 1915

That budded chestnut branch --
        I may be dead,
Ere in the Spring its leaves are fully spread.

Cranleigh
1/12/15

Vain Regret

I dreamed that I was dead;
That on my staring eyes
The earth lay, bitter on my lips and cold,
That o'er my head
Heedless the living trod. I wished to rise;
The hateful clay forbade, and kept its hold.

I wept for very grief
That I was stiff and dead,
That I had thrown away a life so sweet
Beyond belief;
That still all lovely things above my head
Men saw, who on my grave set heedless feet.

Cranleigh
1/12/15

[pages cut out after this poem]

Chance Memory

I can't forget the lane that goes from Steyning to the Ring
In summer time, and on the Down how larks and linnets sing
High in the sun. The wind comes off the sea, and Oh the air! —
I never knew till now that life in old days was so fair.
But now I know it in this filthy rat-infested ditch,
When every shell must kill or spare, and God alone knows which.
And I am made a beast of prey, and this trench is my lair:-
My God! I never knew till now that those days were so fair.
And we assault in half an hour, and -- it's a silly thing,
I can't forget the lane that goes from Steyning to the Ring[6].

"Daily Telegraph"
2/12/15

---

6   Deleted text reads 'narrow lane to Chanctonbury Ring'.

To Cranleigh
Valedictory

Were I to be remembered by a word
To all you here,
One word of all I said or wished to say,
If earth's last day
Came to me on a sudden, as it may:

Were I to be remembered by a deed,
In days to be,
Which might be unforgot, whate'er befall,
Amongst you all,
What word or deed would I have you recall?

Look past all imperfection of my speech
Or ill-done deed;
Think only, there was one who loved you well,
Yet could not tell
How great that love was, till the day he fell.

The Cranleighan
12/18

False Fires

Love is a glamour in a lover's eyes,
A golden dust lit with delusive fires,
Which as a halo lies
About the one whose favour he desires.

Yet can it not abide;

For when the lover late is wise
And his false flame expires,
Only the dust, the bitter dust remains,
To mock the fool for all his fruitless pains.

11/3/16

Early copy adds
Love clasped a statue to his heart, and died,
Since living warmth in marble would not rise.

Idolatria

One narrow path, well worn,
Traced to the thicket's heart,
Secret, in everlasting mould
Of loveliness, is set
The naked image of a fair slim boy,
And on the pedestal shines gold
'TO LOVE AND FORMER JOY';
And briars all the way beset,
Each thorn a sharp regret.

Here often there will come
One to the pedestal
And let some flowers fall
Gently about the feet of that white boy,
Silent, as in regret.

So are wreaths strewn o'er some departed joy.
Or on the lovely head
Of someone that is dead,
When longing in the springtime rouses yet,
In autumn mute regret.

10/3/16

A Wayfaring[7]

What was it that he saw? Who shall now tell[8]
What voice he heard
That he went silent on so long a way,
Sending no word
To one of all of us who loved him well?

Youth's vision, cares of warfare, it may be,
Possessed his soul,
Or as a star rider high and single, he,
To some far goal
Passed where his fate called, not perceiving me.

10/3/16

---

7   'Passage' written in margin.

8   'say' crossed out.

To J.R.E
Understanding

Friend, every man must be, in his own soul,
The builder of his sanctuary of God,
No two of like form, though adorned and whole;
This he may[9] hold, although our diverse minds
Stood[10] wide as pole from pole.

If in a time which may be yet for me,
You cannot judge, did my work stand complete,
Or did my weakness, something to be blamed,
Mar what was otherwise a lovelier shrine,
Let love decide the measure that you mete;
Still think the best of me.

Think that while yet the warm life filled my frame
I made my journey on a worthy quest,
Halting perhaps but hoping all the same,
For what is fine and noble, what is best.
Learning by pain[11] & sympathy to love,
Learning how full of beauty and joy is life.

Think of our former fair companionings,
Our friendships and the journeys we have made;
Think that I had some vision of high things
And loved all beauty that the earth displayed
Or promised me; and think that every soul
Comes through long wand'ring, happy at the last
To one far[12] goal.

28/5/16

---

9   'might' also handwritten.
10   'Stood' added in manuscript.
11   '+ sorrow' added in manuscript.
12   'fair' added in manuscript.

The Dread[13]

When some day shall bring peace, and break the dread
Shall lift from overhead
The daily menace like a thread-hung death;
When peace comes to you as the silence falls,
With stillness that appals
After long beating[14] of a terrible sound.

What will you feel? A joy which leaps beyond
All reason, every bond
Of your restraint, how clamorous and wild?
Or feel life empty for the loss of some
Who now can never come
Back to their places in the pleasant sun?

Or shunning others' joy shall tear apart
A sorrow in your heart
To throb & ache through time without relief:
All that was lovely dead, you living yet
Not hoping to forget
And weary, weary, weary to the end?

28/5/16

---

13 'Peace' in margin.
14 'Pulsing' added in manuscript.

Exile

We stood, a company of men in arms
Ranked in the open night,
Preparing for some fight
When war shall prove us with its worst alarms;
While overhead the multitude of stars
Swung jewelled from the Eastward round the Pole
Or reached their Western goal.
Silent we stood, as dead, each soul,
And in the pines the night wind breathed and sighed.

And I thought of a greater company,
Which stood as silent then,
Ghosts of dead Englishmen,
Who also in their ranks look up to see
The stars which on their England shine at night,
Denied for ever to their living sight.
So held in foreign earth
The men of English birth
Breathe out, pale exile ghosts, their yearning sigh.

28/5/16

On the way into trenches

The road goes down, and darker yet
Deep from about our feet is set;
Below the village waits,
War's mark upon its gates.
Night hides our further way.

Gone now – and lost, the day's glad light
We left beyond the hill; the night
Is heavy-veiled, and doubt
Shadows our way about.
What morrow to the day?

What on tomorrow's page is set –
Unknown to us; fear and regret
Alike unknown, but this
Our hope & courage is:-
We have done well today.

In front of Kemmel
29/7/16

Gain in Loss

Since life holds so much beauty, some delight
Ever must be forgotten, lost to sight
Of memory, as if a man were dead –
Not altogether lost, if, as 'tis said,
If to a man, death looking in his face
There come indeed, in that last moment's space,
The crowded memories of all his days,
And can he give a welcome that repays
So rich a pleasure from so great a friend
Who crowns a happy life with such an end?

4/9/16

A Choice

I do not care what Heaven is for me
What spotless robe and endless minstrelsy,
If I may keep the England that I know
And roam the hillside when dawn breezes blow,
With feet that shall not stir the flowered heath
Unseen, unshadowed, on the earth beneath.

08/16

To a friend
Recollection

Can you before your eyes in memory bring
Prized happinesses England still our own
Not prized till now? — Ah! But you have not known
The swift deep longing which men feel out here,
Which makes old loves a thousand fold more dear
And floods up sudden from some simple thing.

The little rustle of the trees at morn,
When in dawn-dusk the long battalion swings
Winding along the woodside, sudden brings
Dawns I have seen, when over-shadowed corn
Or English heath and pines the morning breathed.

The big round amber moon above the trees,
Calm in the jewel-clear immensity,
Is that same orb which over Trinity
Some warm June night in wondrous silence rode,
Silence all filled with half-heard melodies,
And little lights upon the river flowed.

A summer sun, a road that climbs a hill,
While in the distance – and some English dale
Is mine again by memory, and we
Again a linked line of lads that sing
Care-free, like youths in some old lovely tale,
Timeless, and so immortal, singing still.

Do lads still sing beside the hedgerow shade,
Brushing the first night dew with homeward feet
When leaf-hid chimneys give blue tremulous spires
Which no breath stirs, from window-twinkling fired,
When evening by the woods is cool and sweet
And murmurous stillness fills th'inviolate glade?

And stars will still remind me of the Wolds,
The width and wonder of a winter's night,
Or give back ev'nings which my memory holds
Precious with friendship, and by th'inward sight
I once again with dear friends dearest days
Shall live, still treading youth's fair open ways.

Yet all those days are very far away
And much here seems so bitter, yet I know –
Which in due time shall all my future show –
All I do now shall consummate each day
I then thought perfect, and each memory
Complete, now marred by importunity.

Millencourt
6/9/16

The last mess in billets

The thought floats unawares into my mind –
"This is the last night here; the moment slips
E'en now from us to the past. What shall we find
Up yonder, you with laughter on your lips,
A misty face beyond the lamp, a gleam
Of eyes beyond the glow, across the shine
Of knives and glass & bottles amber, gold
Or clear as water; Jack, – who next to mine
Stretches his slim brown hand upon the cloth
Towards the delicate stemm'd bubble of glass
Which holds a liquid jewel, red as wrath –
And all of us?

And to your lips move mine,
Answer your laughter, and things spoken pass,
While all the time my heart is whispering
"The last night here. To this loved company
What things tomorrow, if tomorrow be?"
And a commonplace word is said, & the thought takes wing
And is lost beyond in the guns' fierce thundering.

Millencourt/Bazentin
8/9/16

To one at home

"The day goes well for England" High of heart
The men who stormed these hills which now we hold,
Who when the call comes shall be no less bold,
Constant no less to play the manly part.

Beyond the crest where sky and earth-wreck meet
Now from afar we view the promised land,
In hope of that high day when we shall stand
Victors, to view our conquest at our feet.

The day goes well for England. We may fall,
And never see beyond, but all our care
Is, those who follow shall stand victorious there
And England conquer by us after all.

And tell your children, that they think of all
Who died upon these hills nor saw the end
Which their death won, as men glad so to spend
Their life's full treasure at their country's call.
Let this be still the hope that England gives
"No Englishman is dead while England lives".

Before Martinpuich
09/16

Loose Leaf

Violets

These violets came from a far old garden of France,
From a sun-lit bed
By an old brick wall speckled golden & green with moss
And striped by straight-branched jargonelles,
Where all the warm air richly smells
Of violets golden-eyed with petals spread
And drowsily sounds the murmur of spread bees.

They shall bring you the childhood days which as years advance
Still dearer grow,
And the happiness yours beyond all fear of loss;
The garden which was home to you
The innocency there you knew.

Undated

To R.N.A
To a Cranleighan

Be sure that if my soul, when flesh-released,
Shall find its dearest liberties increased,
More free to wonder & more strong to love,
Here shall I wonder, and not here the least.

If in some moment of a day to be
You feel a presence which you cannot see,
Familiar though and friendly, then believe
That near you, though unseen, you still have me.

Then if my love has helped you in your need
Or ever prompted to a nobler deed,
Or from my being any profit came,
Love, understanding, joy in fuller meed;

Be sure then that my shade has found a way
To come back to your side and thus repay
Old happinesses and the love you gave
And hours that raised me by her in my day.

29/9/16

June Evening

Twilight lies on the roses; twilight here
Brings to the fields no sound to interfere
With June in England, still inviolate
Runs the white road; all in this silent sphere
In peace and beauty, as the night grows late.

Silence lies round the hamlet like a lake;
The sightless houses wait till man awake,
Man who has made them, whose death they shall see, –
Beside the highway, which alone I take,
The leaves are still, an ebony filigree.

No thunder of the guns, no scream
Of deadly shard, only the stream
Singing its little, ancient, laughing song,
Columnar poplars black above the gleam
And silent woods that scorn man's right and wrong.

Croft -Neasham
06/16

The Land of France[15]

O pleasant land of France, beloved fields,
Where once my friend and I set happy feet
And proved the joys which life-communion yields
To those whose fellowship is made complete;

Spired cities, dark against the ev'ning sky,
Which gave the lamplit meal, the peace of nights,
Cool river-winding roads by morning light –
O lovely race, O lovely memory!

O cruel land of France, which now I hate,
My friend alone now keeps a share of thee,
By that sharp stroke of late calamity,
Which happier memory may not abate –
O cruel land, O cruel memory!

Redcar?
07/16

---

15 Second stanza marked as if for deletion.

Return (cf Passage)

The star that once rode high and sole, and passed
Beyond the range
Of our horizon, now again appears,
And there is change
And pain for us, but gladness that at last

The star regains its East
Yet had it set
Not to arise,
For us it would have gained a brighter fire,
And in our eyes
Have shone something, leading onward yet.

Catterick
3/12/16

Mors Intempestiva

O not for me the rapture of embrace,
Never to me,
Since in my prime I shall untimely die,
Will granted be
The thrilling conquest of a woman's grace.

O not for me to know my perfect power,
The moment's fire
When flames up to an unenduring height
Youth's rich desire,
When all my youth bursts open like a flower,

No perfect month, – ere such a death as this
Warm with red life
Shall feed my sense with passion to full growth,
And for earliest strife,
Shall crown my body's glory with a kiss.

Catterick
17/12/16

(T.O.L.)
A Trust

No son of mine shall ever bear my name,
So, boyhood's friend of mine,
See that it die not, that the shade of shame
Or false tale spread
Bear it not down, for my sake make it thine
When I am dead.

I would have had my son to be as you –
Though you were not aware –
Like you to love, to suffer and to do
What man may dare,
Face, as you faced, the worst of life or death
Yet not despair

God knows I had been glad enough to live
A little longer, still
Since that and fatherhood are not for me,
So let it be;
Take then, for love's sake, all I have to give
My love and my good will.

These for yourself. And some day tell your son,
Whom once I hoped to see,
It is by loving that earth's best is won,
And that for me –
Who loved you – life was splendid with ideals,
Till life was done.

Catterick
8/12/16

Journey's End

While he had life, he loved to wander wide,
Not in our ways alone,
But his desire sought out Avilion,
Nor sought in vain,
A mystic earth beyond a mystic tide
His soul's domain.

His eyes no longer no longer strain to pierce the cloud
That veils the furthest wave,
He has passed over all his track of sea;
His windswept grave
Holds him content; no grave holds hope more proud
Nor heart more brave.

His journey now is done on hills & seas,
His heart has found its goal.
After the length and hardness of the way
His toil is past,
And happy in his far Hesperides
He rests at last.

Catterick
8/12/16

Schoolboys, 1916

You question eagerly to learn of us,
Who come and go
From war to you and back to war again,
And feeling there is much we will not tell,
You seek to know the worst things of that hell.
O be content to leave the matter so;
Thank God you do not know.

Yet should you comprehend the whole
Disastrous woe
And at some future day should have to choose
Whether 'tis life or honour that you lose,
Then in a quarrel which offends your soul[16],
If it be so,
Thank God that you can go.

Cranleigh
09/16

---

16   Deleted text reads 'is not your ???'.

Morituri

We stand beside the gate,
As men who must await
A summons to some terrible beyond,
Whence some return no more,
And none such as before –
If not in body, somewhere hurt in mind.
When we pass through, what fortune shall we find?
Men of no hope nor future, with no claim
Certain on life, who may not aim
Save at an unseen mark.
      And on each brow
Is set in characters invisible now
Sure doom for him who bears but shall not see,
Death & a sudden horror though it be.

Cranleigh
09/16

Untitled

life has been like a journey of the sun
As bright, as brief,
That seems at ending but so late begun
That there is grief
To find, noon passed so soon, its course is run.

The Blessed Isle
An old Sailor Speaks

In glimpses we have seen it o'er the heaving of the sea,
At the sunset & the dawning, & our landfall it shall be.
In our long and weary journeys to the burden of the day
From the tops of hills we've seen it, & it's very far away.
O it's far away and misty & the sea is very wide
But some say we shall reach it when we pass beyond the tide.

And sometimes it seems nearer, & sometimes it is far,
And sometimes come faint breezes from the apple trees there are
By the cool and pleasant waters, & the blossoms that they bring,
A clean sweet smell of meadow land, and oh then how we long
For its fields & trees & flowers & the little birds that sing,
For the old things & the lost things & the memories that cling.

But we're getting nearer, nearer, in the storm & in the fair,
On a life of high adventure, till we find our haven there.
And there's peace there & there's friends there, & there's happiness for all
Who are heavy & are broken & are ready for the call
Which will come to us most likely at the setting of the sun,
For the way is long & weary & we're glad when it is done.

9/12/16

Requiem

Perhaps when all the clamour and heat of strife,
The searing cloud sweeps past,
And after so much troubling and unrest,
Peace wraps me round at last,
Contented I, since I have won earth's best,
Shall rest, for ever rest,
By those tall pines that crown the seaward crest,
And listen happy there
To every wind that moves the clean sweet air,
Warmed by the sun that was my joy in life.

20/7/16

Longing

There is nothing but longing on earth
To the day that we die;
All our longing in pleasure has birth,
Joy ends in a sigh
And content is a thing of no worth.

We desire what we never can gain
From the first to the last;
We are memory-bound by a chain
To the life that is past;
What we had we would have yet again.

Heart-weary, we long for our rest,
For the end of the way,
For the night that brings calm in the breast
Sore vexed by the day
For the dreamless long sleep that is best.

01/17

Opportunity

Haste, haste, to drain the goblet brimming up
With sweet red life, lest cold death's judging hand
Dash down the pleasure to the thirsty sand
Before thy lips have fairly kissed the cup,

And thou go thirsty to thy long chill sleep,
Unlit by star or moon, with grief for mate,
Thou ineffectual ghost, to wish (too late)
That when the cup was thine thou hadst drunk deep.

15/1/17

A Builder

Gone – one who has built Cranleigh, by whose life
Of faithful love,
Strong patience, she makes good his splendid hopes,
Who last, above
His former labour, ended in this strife.

She will be mindful of him, for his death
Completes his toil
Is his last gift to those who knew him there,
Who will not spoil
His work to build while he still had breath.

1/6/17

The Tourists' Complete Guide to the Battlefields
High Wood[17]

Ladies and gentlemen, this is High Wood,
Called by the French, Bois des Fourneaux,
The famous spot which in Nineteen-Sixteen,
July, August and September was the scene
Of long and bitterly contested strife,
By reason of its High commanding site.
Observe the trees - this wire - here was a trench
For months inhabited, contested too,
Heavily shellled, used later as a grave.
It has been said on good authority
That in the fighting for this patch of wood
Were killed somewhere about 8000 men,
Of whom the greater part are buried here,
This mound on which you stand being --
Madame, please,
You are requested kindly not to touch
Or take away the Company's property
As souvenirs; you'll find we have on sale
A great variety, all guaranteed.
As I was saying, all is as it was,
Pray follow me this way.
The path, sir, please.
This is an unknown British officer;
The tunic having lately rotted off
The ground, which was secured at great expense
The Company keeps absolutely untouched,
And in that dug-out (genuine) we provide
Refreshments at a reasonable rate.
You are requested not to leave about
Paper, or ginger beer bottles, or orange peel,
There are waste-paper baskets at the gate.

Humbercamps, 2/6/17

---

17   On loose leaf in the notebook. Inscribed on the back of the poem: 'GBP killed – June 8,
1917. News brought June 16' Published in the 'Nation' 2.6.17.

Blackbirds at Evening

When at the restful ending of the day,
Thinking of old past happy memories,
You hear some treetop blackbird serenade
Against a jewel sky the sinking fire
And (as will come at sunset) you are sad
For memories which with no time will fade;
Think too that far away
One rests, his work well done,
And in the peaceful beauty where he lies
Hears the familiar song which clouds your eyes
And thinks, like you, of all the joy he had
As evening later fell
He homeward coming when the young limbs tire,
To make his meal & glow with family love.
And your thought comes to his, who loved you so
And lies at peace there, smiling, & is glad.

16/7/17

Veterans

Oh we have lived into another age
And even the comrades of our century die
Suffered too much to suffer any more,
Dulled with deep horrors and familiar so
With hopeless disappointment that today
No disappointed hope can make us sore
Though we fend off our sadness in the day,
At evening in the stillness it gets home.
Oh! Oh! For longing that can never be!
Oh for the men our friends who died last year,
Who walked with us in England but of late
And now are with the sleepers of the Somme.

-/7/17

Bairnsfathers[18]

To you Old Bill and Bert
Are just a thoughtless matter for a jest,
Music hall Tommies, "sporting", never sad,
With some pert vulgar quip[19] at death & mud.
You cannot know that one will jest at shells
Which seek him, just because he must, for fear.
But for us
Old Bill and Bert are all our friendships dead
The best companions that man ever had,
And for the rest,
Old suffering stamped deep upon the face
The world a wary, empty, hopeless place.

07/17

---

18   Deleted 'Old Bill'.
19   'Quip' replaces 'jest' – deleted.

At Humbercamps

Out from my window gazing to the North
Into a peace of trees and shadowed street
Veiled in perfection of a July night.
Where distant solitary feet
Echo to mark the stillness, and the trees
Keep a soft ceaseless hushing, I look forth
Beyond confined horizons, and am free
To follow where my swift thoughts take their flight
Northward, — oh cruel north,
Where in a similar calm the Belgian breeze
Breathes so among the leaves —
To take my stand above him who is dead
And speak as if he lay upon his bed,
And he in turn speaks whispering to me:
"All day must you go restless to and fro
"Busied, unsatisfied
"And feeling so much unachieved, still go
"At night to rest which morning will frustrate,
"Uncertain of the least of things to come
"And open to the slightest blow of Fate.
"Contentless even that you feel the sun
"And that warm human blood ...

18/07/17

In Memoriam
Fragments

I will not grieve him as untimely dead,
Nor yet upbraid
The Hand that took him; I can yet believe
That unafraid
He faced the instant peril, that his head

Bowed not, nor did the level of his eyes
Tremble or fall
Before the menace of Death's fronting[20] gaze
And best of all,
That as a fighter to the last he lies.

He might have lived, but that he did not choose
For that great day
To leave the men whose friend & leader he;
The better way
So gain is most when most he seems to lose.

07/17

---

20   Possibly 'frosting'.

Additional Poem on loose paper and handwritten. Given by Rev Elizabeth Jackson 7 June 2022 during her visit to the Borthwick Institute.

A Crucifix at Courcelles

The cross which I behold he once passed by, all unaware
That this road was his way to Calvary,
That he must share
As crucified for us that agony;

Nor knowing that the passion emblems there,
The nails, the reed,
The spear, are types of what it shall be his
With unwatched speed,
After his own Gethsemane, to bear.

And more: shrapnel for nails and spear; no reed
With opiate drink
To dull the torment of the three days' thirst;
He may not shrink
Nor find a comforter in hour of need.

On either side, no thief, but slaughtered friends,
Which his hands find,
And rats. But more. Not helpless only; blind,
— O Christ! — blind, blind.
An agony which no ninth hour death ends.

[21]O not for nothing on that lonely head
Did these things fall;
Nor by chance cruelty of fate, on one
Beloved of all.
He also, shall he not rise from the dead?
For he has lain his time in Hell, and came
Purged by its pain,
And when he leads us in Emmaus' ways
Alive again,
Do not our hearts burn in us like a flame?

6/5/17

---

21   This stanza marked 'x' as if for deletion.